'I was never to see my friend again. Before those leaves had turned and fallen he was snatched by an assassin's bullet.'

Harold Macmillan

Kennedy at Birch Grove

Paul Elgood

To Lee, who shared the many journeys

First Published 2012

ISBN-13: 978-1467996549

ISBN-10: 1467996548

© All rights reserved by Paul Elgood.

Author Blog and contact details at
www.kennedyatbirchgrove.tumblr.com

Contents

Schedule extract for 29th and 30th June 1963	6
Prologue	9
Chapter 1	11
Chapter 2	19
Chapter 3	25
Chapter 4	33
Chapter 5	39
Chapter 6	47
Chapter 7	55
Epilogue	59
Appendix	61

Schedule extract from the John F. Kennedy Library for 29th and 30th June 1963

Saturday, June 29th 1963

5.30pm President John F. Kennedy arrived at Gatwick Airport, Gatwick, England and makes a short address

5.53pm The President and Prime Minister depart Gatwick Airport by helicopter and flew to Birch Grove house, Chelwood Gate

6.08pm Arrival at Birch Grove house

8.00pm Small dinner at Birch Grove in honor of President Kennedy

No. 276

PRESIDENT KENNEDY'S VISIT

BIRCH GROVE HOUSE

June 29 and 30, 1963

Security Passes for Gatwick Airport and Birch Grove House, June 29th and 30th 1963 (author's collection).

Sunday, June 30th 1963

8.15am President Kennedy departed Birch Grove house to attend Our Lady of the Forest Church, Forest Row

9.25am The President returns to Birch Grove and undertakes a photo opportunity with Prime Minister Harold Macmillan

12.00 noon small luncheon

3.15pm The President and Prime Minister depart Birch Grove for Gatwick Airport

3.30pm Arrival at Gatwick Airport and inspection of honor guard

3.45pm The President departs Gatwick for Malpensa Airport

> **No. 128**
> **GATWICK AIRPORT**
> **President Kennedy's Visit**
> Please admit bearer to Reception Area for
> ARRIVAL — June 29, 1963
> DEPARTURE — June 30, 1963

Prologue

At the height of the Cold War, the eyes of the world turned briefly to a quiet corner of the English countryside.

On 29th June 1963, America's youthful and charismatic 35th President, John F. Kennedy, paid a flying visit to the East Sussex countryside to meet British Prime Minister, Harold Macmillan, at his country house, Birch Grove. The short stopover followed two of Kennedy's most famous overseas visits as President - Berlin and Ireland. After just 24 hours Kennedy would leave England never to return, on his way to Italy and the final leg of his historic four-nation European tour. Both men would face difficult months ahead leading to resignation for Macmillan in October and for Kennedy, who tragically lost a child just weeks later, they led ultimately to the dramatic events of November 22nd 1963.

Birch Grove acted as the stage for 24 hours of talks between the two men, with all the comings and goings of an international Cold War summit.

Although rural East Sussex had not seen anything similar to a Presidential visit before, the weekend of 29th and 30th June 1963, unlike the unfolding historic events in Berlin or the crowd-stopping motorcades in Dublin and Rome has become a footnote in the history books; a short Presidential stopover, designed to keep the British as close allies and let Kennedy spend a night in the English countryside en route to Rome.

Macmillan saw the 'thrilling' 24 hours as 'fantastic, even romantic'[1] and although brief, this near-forgotten moment of Presidential history offers an enthralling insight into Anglo-American relations during the raised tensions of the Cold War. It is also the story of America as superpower and Britain coming to terms with its international decline.

Using the original files from the time and Macmillan's own account, this short history pieces together those hours at Birch Grove 50 years on.

"HYA, MAC — HOW ARE YOU KEEPING?"

Victor Weisz, Evening Standard, 28 July 1963

Chapter One

It was JFK calling. As David Powers walked into room 359 of Brighton's Grand Hotel, the bedside telephone was ringing. Picking it up, Powers was met by the frustrated voice of President John F. Kennedy thirty miles away at the country house of English Premier, Harold Macmillan, demanding to know why his senior aide had sneaked out of Birch Grove whilst he was dressing for dinner. At the first opportunity Powers had headed down to the coast, where he had planned a relaxing evening with the crew of Air Force One at the Sussex seaside resort. The crew, press and US communications staff had been forced to decamp to the seaside resort due to the lack of hotel space in the Birch Grove area and Powers had the option on a hotel room at the Grand Hotel as well as at the country house. 'I suppose you've been cooking up this little party for a week or more,' Kennedy roared down the phone, more upset at missing out on the Saturday night fun than not having his advisor close at hand during the evening's dinner and subsequent discussions with Macmillan. Kennedy would later ring back to demand Power's presence first thing the next morning when he planned to attend mass in Forest Row. In the end though, he would be making the trip to mass without Powers the next morning.[2]

President John F. Kennedy arrived at Gatwick Airport, then a small airstrip south of London, at 5.28pm on Saturday 29th June 1963.[3] The adoring and magical crowds of Ireland, where he charmed the nation and famously promised to 'return in the springtime' must have seemed long behind him by then. Advisor Kenneth O'Donnell would later recall his four day tour as the happiest of Kennedy's life, and that the emotional trip to the 'land of the Kennedys' was one of the defining events of his abbreviated presidency.[4] Crowds flocked to see his every move as he toured Galway, Dublin and Cork in his open-top Cadillac, open and accessible to those who came to see, even touch him. Euphoria seemed to engulf Ireland and Kennedy's rock star anointment was the coming of age for this young nation, after breaking free from the long dark days of its colonial master. In reality though his remarks at the Dáil were less well received and upset Irish President, De Valera. Macmillan, in retrospect, also thought Kennedy's speech 'rather foolish'.

Berlin, the first stop on his four-nation tour gave Kennedy the opportunity to confront the Soviets and re-affirm that the city and its people would again be free. The newly built wall had divided the city and became, in effect, the world's frontline. Kennedy wanted to rally the people of West Berlin, making one of the most historic speeches of his presidency and warning those who thought Communism worked to 'come to Berlin' and see the divided city for themselves. The speech, and in particular its location in the free part of the city, was a calculated risk for Kennedy however the response it was met with paid dividends. Like Ireland, massive crowds had received Kennedy as a rock star, showering his car with flowers and standing for hours waiting for the motorcade to pass momentarily. Kennedy showed them that the people of West Berlin were not alone and that the free world would defend their city and its frontline. Today people are more used to charismatic young leaders grabbing attention on the world stage, but Kennedy had followed the likes of Presidents Eisenhower and Truman from a different era of politics – Kennedy was the first President of the rock and roll age. Back then they simply had not seen anything like it.

President John F. Kennedy needs little introduction as an American political and cultural icon of the 1960s. Born into wealth and privilege Kennedy was pressed by his father, Ambassador Joseph P. Kennedy to pursue a career in politics immediately after he left the Navy at the end of the Second World War. In 1946 Kennedy won a seat in Congress from his home city of Boston, giving him that first, essential foothold on the path to the Presidency. Never said to be particularly suited to the House of Representatives, Kennedy quickly eyed the Massachusetts US Senate seat then held by Henry Cabot Lodge, an elder statesman of the Republican Party. In an otherwise off year for Democrats, Kennedy sensationally defeated Cabot Lodge, taking his place in the Senate on the first attempt. After arriving in the Senate, Kennedy's reputation began to grow, even though ill-heath meant that on a number of occasions he was forced to spend time away from politics. By 1956 though, he had challenged for the Vice Presidency, and whilst unsuccessful that time, he was able to settle for a well-received nominating speech at the convention, viewed by millions across the country. From that moment on, Kennedy vigorously pursued the Presidency.

Kennedy's journey through the 1960 Democratic primaries was far from assured. Hubert Humphrey, Adlai Stevenson and Lyndon Johnson all eyed the nomination, knowing 1960 to be the best opportunity to defeat the Republicans since 1948. In the primaries Kennedy took to the road and campaigned extensively across the primary states. Kennedy's image as a rich playboy does not reflect the campaigning skill and energy he put into winning his seats in the House of Representatives and US Senate and later the Democratic nomination for the Presidency. Indeed, Kennedy represented a working class district of Boston when a congressman and seemed at home there. The Kennedy approach for each election was similar, to win them person by person, through an endless stream of factory gates, walkabouts and tea parties. It became a family operation with his brother Bobby Kennedy running the campaign and other family members either based out in the field or hosting the famous Kennedy family tea parties. Kennedy's early success in the primaries made him the candidate to beat, however questions still persisted about whether a rich Catholic boy could carry the nation against the likely Republican nominee, Vice President, Richard Nixon.

The primary campaigns reached a climax in West Virginia, with its white working class majority. If Kennedy, a wealthy Catholic, could win there, he could win the nation. Kennedy addressed the Catholic issue head-on and by polling day beat Humphrey 69% to 31%, and with it, effectively sewed-up the primaries. Learning from the mistakes of the 1956 Democratic Convention, when he lost the Vice Presidency, partly due to poor convention floor organisation, in 1960, Bobby Kennedy took charge of herding the delegates, and partly as a result, Kennedy was subsequently nominated as Presidential candidate.

The 1960 Presidential campaign is perhaps best remembered for the first televised debates between the candidates. The story goes that radio listeners preferred the policy detail of Richard Nixon, but that television viewers were more taken with Kennedy's youthful good looks against Nixon's pale on-screen persona. Kennedy had become the master of the television age, something which would carefully craft his image in the White House. The election would go down to the wire, with Kennedy narrowly beating Nixon in the November election, and subsequently elected to the Presidency at just 43 years of age. Kennedy's breathtaking oratory at his inaugural began his thousand days in the White House, but as President, Kennedy would meet adversity as well as opportunity. He learnt an early lesson with the failed Bay of Pigs landing, but was more confident by the time of the Cuban Missile Crisis, where his assured and steady approach avoided the potential for nuclear confrontation. By June 1963 Kennedy had one eye on re-election, and his historic visits to Berlin and Ireland had begun to cement his image internationally and at home.

The pace of Kennedy's European tour that summer slowed after Dublin as he arrived in England, with newspapers of the time reporting that Kennedy would 'slip into the country almost unnoticed...' on the Saturday afternoon.[5] Arriving in this way gave Kennedy the opportunity to pay his respects to a member of his family privately: his sister Kathleen. Instead of flying directly from Dublin to Gatwick, Kennedy had first detoured to Chatsworth House in Derbyshire to the grave of his sister who had married Anglican, Billy Hartington, son and heir of the Duke of Devonshire. Kennedy had not attended the funeral or visited her grave before, as he had turned back whilst travelling to the funeral, it was said too upset to continue. The detour in 1963 gave Kennedy his only opportunity to pay his respects to his lost sister, who had died in an air crash over France in 1948. At the grave he paid his respects in private, away from the public glare. The link through marriage with the Devonshire family also gave Kennedy a notable connection with the Macmillan family, through Harold's wife, Dorothy Macmillan who was the daughter of the ninth Duke and Duchess of Devonshire. Perhaps not since Georgian times had the governing families of America and England been so intertwined.

Even in 1963, it took a staggering amount to move a President. Schedules from the time show the arrival of three jumbo jets, which due to the length of the runway, was the first time modern jumbo jets had landed at Gatwick. Kennedy had first used the powder-blue Boeing 707 SAM 26000 jet in November 1962, after Jacqueline Kennedy repainted the plane's colours to those still familiar today and removed its drab army markings to create the icon of American Presidential power. To add to the mystique of the new plane public mention of its now familiar code name, Air Force One, was allowed for the first time during Kennedy's Presidency. Just a few months later the same aircraft would carry Kennedy's casket back to Washington from Dallas after his assassination, and would be the scene of Lyndon Johnson's historic swearing-in on the tarmac at Love Field Airport.[6] The plane would receive tight, round-the-clock security at Gatwick whilst waiting for the President, and be ready to depart at short notice, should the need arise.

Visits to Britain by sitting American Presidents took place far less often than today. President Barack Obama visited both in 2009 and 2011, and George W. Bush travelled to the United Kingdom five times during his two-term Presidency. President Woodrow Wilson was the first sitting American President to visit England in 1918; his trip included an excursion to Carlisle, where his family originated. Harry Truman was the next President to visit in 1945, and then Dwight Eisenhower in 1959. As President, Kennedy had previously been to London in 1961 for a private family christening, and was received by the Queen. Kennedy had known London well from his father's time as ambassador in the run-up to the Second World War. The 1961 visit caused as much interest as subsequent overseas visits by Kennedy, especially as the

First Lady joined him. Surprisingly, Lyndon Johnson did not visit the UK during his term in office, even though the period was dominated by foreign affairs, and it took until Richard Nixon's visit in 1969 for a sitting President to return after Birch Grove.[7] Until Bill Clinton, as a Rhodes Scholar, no other twentieth century President had spent so much time in England.

Kennedy was no stranger to England. As United States Ambassador to London, or the Court of St James, his father Joseph P. Kennedy, lived in London in the run-up to the Second World War. The Kennedy family followed, with John F. Kennedy travelling across England and indeed Europe in the run-up to the war. Will Smith writes, in his account of their time in pre-war London, 'The Kennedys amidst the Gathering Storm' that:

> 'Jack Kennedy used his father's tenure in Europe to travel widely and satisfy his enormous curiosity about other political system and cultures…and help create an identity as an internationalist American.'[8]

John F. Kennedy first arrived in London in July 1938, and as Swift puts it, 'blazed a seductive path through social and aristocratic London'.[9] Taking advantage of his family's new position in London's elite, Kennedy who admired Winston Churchill even attended the House of Commons to hear his hero speak from the public gallery. It was during this period that he developed lasting Anglo-American friendships, most significantly with future British Ambassador to Washington, David Ormsby-Gore, who Swift describes as acting as a 'wiser older brother'. These formative relationships would later prove vital to him in foreign relations as he set about establishing his administration in 1961. Ormsby-Gore would offer wise and cautious counsel to Kennedy when it came to Cold War diplomacy. For Kennedy and Macmillan, Birch Grove would be their seventh meeting during their terms in office; previous meetings included a visit to Washington DC and a summit in Nassau. At each of these Kennedy and Macmillan increased their friendship.

Chapter Two

The British welcoming party at Gatwick had to wait patiently in the rain for Kennedy and his entourage to finally arrive. The first of the three jumbo jets to land at the airport carried two bubble-top motorcade cars for the President; the second plane was Air Force One 26000 itself and the third was the back-up plane, which always accompanied the President in case of emergency. Two US Army helicopters acted as shuttles for the short journey between Gatwick and Birch Grove; two more RAF 225 squadron whirlwind helicopters were used to ferry the press and staff to hotels and to a US government communications base in Brighton, using the Brunswick Lawns on the seafront as a landing site.

The President's party was considerable and included his Secretary of State, Dean Rusk and McGeorge Bundy, Special Assistant to the President for National Security. Press Secretary, Pierre Salinger, O'Donnell, Powers, Kennedy's Secretary, Mrs Evelyn Lincoln, his doctor and valet plus communication and security personnel accompanied Kennedy.

As Secretary of State, Dean Rusk was first appointed to government by President Truman in 1949, and was America's top diplomat through the entire Kennedy and Johnson administrations, during the events of the Bay of Pigs, the Cuban Missile Crisis, and the building of the Berlin Wall through to Johnson's failed intervention in Vietnam. Rusk would eventually leave the post as the second longest serving Secretary of State in history. Rusk came directly from Berlin and left early for Rome, having been in London for the two days prior to Kennedy's arrival. National Security Advisor, McGeorge Bundy, also served both Kennedy and Johnson, but resigned in 1966. As part of Kennedy's White House inner circle, Bundy was one of the 'best and the brightest' Kennedy used for advice on foreign policy.

The British welcoming party at Gatwick, waiting for the delayed Americans, was more modest. Foreign Secretary, Lord Home, British Ambassador to Washington and lifelong Kennedy friend, Sir David Ormsby-Gore and Downing Street Private Secretary, Mr Philip de Zulueta joined Prime Minister Macmillan to greet the President. The Lord Lieutenant of Surrey, the Earl Munster represented the Queen during the proceedings and two detectives completed the welcoming line-up.

The term 'old school' could well have been invented for Harold Macmillan. Born into England's Victorian landed gentry, to a famed publishing family, Macmillan rose steadily through the ranks of the Conservative Party. First elected to Parliament in the 1920s, Macmillan lost his seat three times, finally settling on the outer London borough of Bromley as his final constituency in Parliament. Macmillan held successive posts in the Churchill and Eden governments, serving as Defence Secretary, Foreign Secretary and Chancellor, were among the string of government offices he held during his long progression to power. He was perhaps best remembered as Minister for Housing under Churchill where he reached the challenging target of building 300,000 new homes each year to meet the rising demand in post war Britain. Following Anthony Eden's resignation in 1957, in the wake of the Suez debacle, the Queen called on Macmillan to form a government, choosing him over his long-standing Cabinet colleague, Rab Butler. It seemed a good choice at the time. Macmillan increased the Conservative majority in the 1959 General Election, which was held during a period of economic growth and prosperity, and about which Macmillan would be best remembered for his 'never had it so good' remark. By 1963, the Macmillan government was struggling and seen as out of touch, with the Profumo scandal undermining the reputation of his government. Secretary of Defence John Profumo had been exposed for conduct viewed as unbecoming to his government post and which raised serious national security issues. At the time of the Birch Grove meeting Macmillan was heavily tainted by the scandal, even though history would show both men to be inherently honourable and honest.

Alec Douglas-Home, by that time effective Prime Minister in waiting, was another aristocratic Tory in the same vein as Macmillan. In October 1963 he would succeed Macmillan as the Conservative choice against Labour's Harold Wilson in the 1964 General Election. By aligning itself even more closely with the traditional landed gentry, the Conservative Party of the era showed itself to be increasingly out of step with the changing times. Both Macmillan and Home were decent men and one-nation Conservatives, but their governments were tainted by scandal and out of touch with the social changes of the decade. Harold Wilson, of course, represented the changing population of that time, in the same way Labour had before in 1945 and would again in 1997.

Sir David Ormsby-Gore could perhaps have joined either the welcoming or visiting delegations. A close friend of the Kennedy family since their time in London when Joseph P. Kennedy was the controversial US Ambassador to the Court of St. James, Ormsby-Gore was even distantly related to the Kennedy family. He played a significant role in the Cuban Missile Crisis acting as the link between the two governments. During the raised tensions, Ormsby-Gore was one of Kennedy's sources for illegal Cuban cigars, specially imported via the embassy courier bags! He would go on to be one of Robert Kennedy's pallbearers in 1968.

The arrival scene at Gatwick's south extension mirrored that of other visits by overseas dignitaries: the compulsory inspection line, military band and brief remarks of welcome from both sides. The youthful Kennedy stood adjacent to the older Macmillan, highlighting the contrast between the old and new world orders: Macmillan, the last British Prime Minister to be born in the nineteenth century; Kennedy, the first American President to be born in the twentieth century. Kennedy's pre-written arrival remarks set out the discussions the leaders would have on the international tensions facing the East and West. Formalities over, they departed for Birch Grove, with Macmillan catching a ride in the President's helicopter whilst Rusk and Home were driven, with a police escort.

Kennedy and Macmillan had differing motives for the visit. In many ways for Kennedy it was simply a brief respite after the visits to Berlin and Ireland, whilst he waited for the enthronement of the new Pope in Rome. Kennedy dared not undertake such a high profile tour of Europe, without stopping in England first. Macmillan, whose government was deeply embroiled in scandal and drastically lagged behind in the polls was desperate for the domestic boost, which the popular Kennedy's presence would bring. For months now, Macmillan's Tory government had been on the ropes, dogged by scandal and out of touch with the fast moving social changes of the early sixties. Macmillan fitted more easily into the role of Edwardian statesman than that of new world leader that Kennedy so encompassed. French newspapers reported it as a snub to President De Gaulle by Kennedy not visiting France during his four nation tour, even though his previous visit there was such a success. Kennedy would have been conscious that he could not cause similar offence to his friend, Macmillan.

White House files held in the John F. Kennedy Library warn the President of the cul-de-sac in which the scandal-ridden British administration was increasingly finding itself. Kennedy had developed a friendly and genial relationship with the older Macmillan, a bond which he had not been able to develop with other older leaders of the time, including former Presidents Truman and Eisenhower who, during the 1960 election campaign had judged him too young and lacking in experience to run for President. Kennedy knew that he could not undertake a high profile tour of Europe without at least a courtesy call to Macmillan, and a private visit to his country estate reflected the significance of their friendship to him. Kennedy also needed to slow his pace after exhausting days in Berlin and Ireland and had to make sure his arrival in Italy and then Rome was after the new Pope was enthroned.

On landing at Gatwick, White House phone lines were connected to Air Force One, in case the President needed to contact Washington before disembarking. Even though their time at Gatwick was limited, a special press marquee was also set up, and included 30 acoustic telephone booths, which in the event were hardly used. Attention was even given to which flags were flying, and who supplied them.

With formalities at Gatwick over, the Birch Grove police log records that Kennedy arrived at the house at 6pm, flying into the specially installed temporary helicopter pad next to the Macmillan estate. Macmillan describes the welcome in his dairies:

> 'In our immediate neighbourhood the excitement was intense, and the impression left was lasting. To greet Kennedy on his arrival I invited children from neighbouring schools, neighbours, tenants, servants and estate staff... The roads were packed outside the front gate... All seemed to be inspired by a single spirit. To them, Kennedy meant youth, energy, idealism and a new hope for the world.'[10]

Even with the numerous high profile comings and goings of Macmillan's country estate over the years, Birch Grove and the surrounding area was literally the focus of the world, for that day.

The private meetings between the leaders would reflect the times in which they lived. Having been to Berlin, and seen for himself the divided city, and with the Cuban Missile Crisis less than a year behind them, Kennedy's overseas policy centred on East-West tensions and limiting the growth of missiles, which Macmillan was keen to see as a joint initiative between the countries. The agenda for the various sessions at Birch Grove included a world tour of trouble spots of the time, both from a UK and US perspective.

Chapter Three

Situated on the edge of Ashdown Forest, Birch Grove was the only home Macmillan saw truly as his own. Built by his parents, in particular his mother Helen (known as 'Nellie') Macmillan developed a strong love for the house and its beautiful forest setting, buried deep in thick woodland. Robert Coughlan visited Birch Grove for 'Life Magazine' in 1958, and found the house to be 'mostly Georgian in style, with brick walls and ample windows and stone cornices. It is roomy and solid.' Coughlan added that the house reflected the political personality of its occupant so closely that 'one could imagine it built and ... maintained by the Conservative Party'.[11]

Owning the property since 1906, the Macmillans rebuilt the old manor house on the site in 1926 in a Queen Anne style. The two-storey house was built of brown brick, with two bays and a tall French-style roof. During the war, Birch Grove housed evacuees and for a brief time even became a boarding school. Macmillan eventually re-occupied the house after the war. The house had deep connections with the Macmillan family, with Macmillan's mother overseeing both the re-building of the old manor house, the interior of the new house and the layout of the gardens. Responsibility for the estate passed to Harold, after her death.

The house itself played an important and unique role in post-war British politics, becoming the stage for many of the dramas of Macmillan's political life. During his rise to power, the house became an important venue for Macmillan to meet and entertain guests, something which was useful to his increasing political status. Relatively close to Churchill's country house, Chartwell, and just 38 miles from London, it was ideally located as a centre for post-war Conservative politics, and yet rural enough to be surrounded by the hunting gentry with whom Macmillan identified so strongly. Macmillan was more suited to pre-war England than the by-then swinging sixties. Equally Macmillan's final constituency of Bromley was a convenient stopping-off place on his way to the country. Adjacent to the property is the tiny hamlet of Chelwood Gate, and the small pub now called the Red Lion. To the south east is Horsted Keynes and to the north east, Forest Row. During his premiership, Macmillan welcomed world leaders to the house including General De Gaulle, Eisenhower, Khrushchev and Nehru. It gave the tiny East Sussex hamlet of Chelwood Gate an unusually high profile for such a small rural community.

As the advance White House schedule states, Kennedy was due to arrive at Birch Grove at 5pm, but the local police log confirms his arrival as 6pm, after arriving at Gatwick at 5.28pm, and allowing time for his visit to Chatsworth House and the visit to the grave of his sister. Two US Army helicopters landed at the property, Kennedy and Macmillan in the first. Macmillan recalls the Saturday as a 'nasty wet day'[12] and 'The Times' recounts the developing scene during the weekend:

> 'Except for the 300 policemen, the American security men lurking behind every boulder, police dogs baring their teeth at all the entrances, helicopters hovering overhead and journalists jammed into every telephone box, this could have been any away-from-it-all weekend in the country....'[13]

For some hours Birch Grove and the surrounding area had attracted a raised level of attention and with it in a state of virtual lock-down. With the intense public interest in the Berlin and Dublin legs of the trips, newspapers in London had trailed Kennedy's visit for some days in advance, especially as the stopover provided the only opportunity for the British to glimpse the President during his tour. However, without official opportunities to see the President, interested onlookers had to create their own chances to glimpse him. The police log records two small groups of onlookers trying to gain access to the property at 4.35pm, one pair climbing over the gate by the small lodge house. They were easily deterred and of course neither Kennedy nor Macmillan would have been particularly aware of their presence ahead of their arrival. Small groups of anti-war protestors from CND and the Committee of 100 also mounted a presence at Birch Grove during the weekend, and briefly saw Kennedy as he drove past on Sunday morning. CND needs no introduction here, but the lesser known today and shorter-lived Committee of 100 was formed with signatures from 100 public figures of the day, including philosopher Bertrand Russell to campaign against nuclear armament. The group of protestors probably bemused Kennedy rather than being any particular threat, especially considering their presence deep in the English countryside. In advance of the visit, government files from the time show that the Home Office was concerned that they may attempt to block the road around Birch Grove, and even place a 'dummy bomb close to the President's aircraft or baggage'.

Inside the estate, Kennedy and his immediate group of advisors had been allocated rooms in the main house. Kennedy himself was offered Nellie Macmillan's old bedroom and Macmillan's father's dressing room. Macmillan saw his mother's room as the nicest in the house and one he enjoyed spending time in, so offered it to his guest. Files released from the UK National Archives show that a new double bed had to be delivered to provide firm support for the President's back, although the Americans still had their own mattress and pillows for the President.[14] Macmillan recalls that a '…specially constructed bed had to be brought, on which alone he could get comfort.'[15] Macmillan added a personal touch with a specially purchased rocking chair for Kennedy to use during the summit, which helped ease his back pain during long meetings. Kennedy famously used rocking chairs in the White House, to help relieve the pain, following doctor's advice. Originally a government purchase for the visit, bought by Macmillan, he would treasure the chair for the rest of his life as a reminder of the visit, eventually leaving it in his will.

Wherever a President goes, the machinery of government follows. Even in the 1960s, a small administrative and security army accompanied the President, with the Americans importing all they needed to create a secure bubble around the President. Macmillan describes the scene, by saying:

> 'My own house and my son's were made available; but of course they were not large enough to contain Secretaries of State, Ambassadors, members of the Foreign Office and State Department, secretaries, typists and all the protective apparatus which constituted his immense court.'[16]

British Special Branch officers were responsible for security inside the house and grounds, and the East Sussex constabulary outside the estate, but in reality the US Secret Service controlled the vicinity wherever the President went. Although some US personnel were unarmed, the Americans submitted a list to the Home Office of firearms being carried by protection officers during the visit. All visitors to Birch Grove and their vehicles were issued with special security passes, without which they were unable to gain access.

Kennedy was allocated use of the Birch Grove library as an office, with police files from the time recording that the American Embassy in London delivered two lockable safes to the house for his documents to be secured. Unarmed US Marines in plain clothes guarded the rooms. Kennedy Press Secretary, Pierre Salinger had actually requested that Macmillan give up his bedroom for the President, an unsuccessful demand gently broken to the Prime Minister by his Private Secretary. Five direct lines were installed in the house, which were operated from the White House switchboard in Washington DC with the instructions to the user to 'simply lift the receiver and ask for the person required'; they were adapted to allow for different electrical circuits. A helicopter pad was built and lit all night at the Birch Grove property and an ambulance stood ready in case of a Presidential medical emergency. Special instructions were issued to the communications workers not to damage or mark any woodwork in Birch Grove during the installation of the secure communications cabling.

As in all royal courts, proximity to the President meant everything. Staying in Birch Grove House, Kennedy would be joined by Rusk, Bundy and Secret Service Agent Gerald Behn, with Powers already in Brighton. Instructions for Powers' luggage state that there was a room for him at Birch Grove House and a suite at the Grand Hotel in

Brighton, 'depending on where he wishes to stay'. Confusion over his intended whereabouts was reflected in talks between Salinger and de Zulueta, who refers to Powers as 'a sort of court jester'. Records show that Kennedy's valet, George Thomas would also sleep in the main house, with easy access to the President, to meet his needs. Thomas was Kennedy's longstanding valet, who lived on the third floor of the White House. During Kennedy's early days in Congress the story goes that he would even deliver Kennedy's hot lunch to his office each day. Macmillan, on the other hand, had 'few servants' and had to borrow a butler from the government hospitality department.[17]

US Ambassador Bruce and Mr Tyler stayed in the house of the Prime Minister's son, Maurice Macmillan, also on the Birch Grove estate. As Secretary of State, Rusk was provided with an office over the garage of Maurice Macmillan's house. Rusk had travelled from Gatwick by car with his British opposite number, Alex Douglas-Home. Kennedy's personal secretary, Evelyn Lincoln, and other White House staff assistants stayed in the Ashdown Forest Hotel, to be close at hand if needed.

First Lady, Jacqueline Kennedy had not accompanied the President on his trip to Europe. She was heavily pregnant at the time and stayed in Washington DC, preparing for the birth of what would be their third child, expected just weeks later. It was a source of regret for President Kennedy that his wife did not attend the visit, especially after the success of her presence on previous visits; in Paris, for example, where Jacqueline had quite literally stolen the show. In the coming months Kennedy would ask senior aide, Dave Powers to tell stories to Jacqueline of their trip and the euphoric welcome he received.

Kennedy's sisters, Eunice and Jean had accompanied him in Ireland and to their sibling's grave at Chatsworth.

At all times, an American President is surrounded by a tight security detail. Overseas, this was stretched to the limit, however Birch Grove itself did not cause the same concern that the previous days in Berlin and Ireland would have. Writing in 2010, Secret Service Special Agent, Gerald Blaine called that part of the trip a 'logistical nightmare'.[18] Birch Grove held none of the risks of standing at the Berlin Wall in front of armed East German soldiers or in front of the million people who turned out to hear Kennedy rally free Berlin in the city's Rudolph Wilde Platz on June 26th. However, the Secret Service would have been aware that it would take just one incident to threaten the safety of the President, and this was the only time in England that Kennedy would be open to such an attack. Files show three-way advance discussions between the Secret Service, Home Office and the East Sussex Constabulary for the operation. As stated, in reality both the Home Office and local police were bystanders to the Americans who controlled the direct vicinity wherever the President went. The biggest difficulties the Secret Service faced were the motorcades, and Kennedy's habit of stopping to greet well-wishers on the routes he travelled. However, unlike the big cities of Berlin and Dublin, the English countryside and its narrow country lanes helped to physically restrict the number who could turn out to see the President. Additionally, opportunities to see Kennedy were limited to his brief journey to the church in Forest Row.

Chapter Four

The majority of visitors stayed on the Sussex coast in Brighton, where a US government communications centre had been established. Cut off from Birch Grove, RAF helicopters and Embassy cars provided a link between the two during daylight hours. The helicopter shuttles offered 'rapid transportation for members of the Presidential party and for couriers carrying classified matter'. The visit also led to the closure of Brighton's main seafront road to ensure quick access between the hotels and the helicopter landing sites.

The one hitch in the whole advance organisation was the set-up of the telephone communications link, which provided direct lines to the White House from the helicopter pad on Brunswick Lawns, along the seafront from the Grand Hotel. Each major access point was given a direct line to the White House switchboard, but the cables were only dug on the lawns on the Saturday, with the joining team quickly establishing the secure lines just in time for the arrivals later that evening. The phones were operated from joiner's tents on Hove Lawns, extraordinary considering the need for security.

The Presidential staff stayed in the Grand Hotel, whilst the American and overseas press stayed in the adjacent Metropole Hotel, under the ever-watchful eye of Kennedy press secretary, Pierre Salinger. Salinger had been appointed White House press secretary as part of the incoming Kennedy administration in January 1961. After Kennedy's death, he was retained for a short period by President Johnson, leaving in March 1964. Later in the same year Salinger was appointed by Governor Pat Brown to the US Senate to fill a vacancy in his native California. He lost the subsequent election, but went on to follow a successful career with the ABC television network. A leading Kennedy loyalist, Salinger was within ten feet of Robert Kennedy when he was assassinated in 1968. In his memoirs, Macmillan says that Salinger was joined by his own press secretary, Harold Evans who 'shepherded the press... [which] came and went in great numbers, but caused us no trouble.'[19]

All hotels in the Birch Grove vicinity were booked up by the visit. In the early 1960s, Sussex was, and still is to some degree, a cluster of rural villages bounded by the urban sprawl of outer London to the north, and the coastal conurbations to the south. In Brighton, 118 rooms were formally reserved at the Metropole Hotel alone; another 107 were reserved in the Grand, with a further 16 rooms booked in the Grand for the crew of Air Force One. In total well over 250 rooms were officially booked during the stay, not including those of the Secret Service and local police, or indeed interested hangers-on. US Embassy staff also stayed at the Grosvenor Hotel in London, with the back-up Air Force One crew. The visit gave Brighton a mini-boom in four star hotel room lettings.

Senior Kennedy aides, Ted Sorenson and Kenneth O'Donnell joined Dave Powers at the Grand Hotel. The men formed the intellectual group of senior advisers around the President, and structured much of the work of the administration. As Special Counsel and Adviser to the President, Ted Sorensen was Kennedy's de-facto Chief of Staff, although such a post was not designated in the administration and did not become a permanent fixture in the White House until the Nixon administration. As the lead White House speechwriter, Sorensen also provided the President with the drafts of his speeches, including working on those Kennedy gave in Berlin and Ireland during the earlier stop on the European tour. Sorensen's most famous Kennedy collaboration was the inaugural address in which Kennedy challenged the world to 'ask not'.

Dave Powers, when not being pursued by the President on the phone, was Kennedy's Special Assistant. He, with Kenneth O'Donnell, would accompany Kennedy everywhere he went, and together they would act as his political fixers. Like the Kennedys, Powers came from a Boston Irish American family and first met John Kennedy in 1946 when there was a knock on the door of his Charlestown house: "In the semi-darkness I could see this tall, thin, handsome fellow,' and he reached out his hand and said, 'My name is Jack Kennedy. I am a candidate for Congress. Will you help me?'" That moment proved life-changing for Powers, who followed Kennedy to the White House.[20] Both Powers and O'Donnell would be in the motorcade in Dallas.

Official White House photographer, Cecil Stoughton stayed at the Grand Hotel. Stoughton created many of the iconic photographs which came to define Kennedy's 'Camelot' image and would remain at the White House for the first two years of the Johnson administration. Stoughton was not a member of the press and did not stay in the press hotel, but was retained and 'controlled'[21] by the White House, meaning that all the photographs and negatives he took were government property. His job was to follow Kennedy and photograph his every public and often private move, giving him unique proximity to the President and first family. Stoughton was also in the motorcade in Dallas when Kennedy was shot. Later that day he took the only photograph of President Johnson's swearing-in on Air Force One, on the tarmac in Dallas following the assassination. The swearing-in took place on the same plane Kennedy had come to Europe in earlier that summer, and which was waiting for him at Gatwick whilst he was at Birch Grove.

Kennedy's close friend, Lem Billings also stayed in the Grand Hotel. Since their school days Billings faithfully followed Kennedy wherever he went and was among the most loyal of the Kennedy loyalists. A New York advertising executive by profession, Billings had free access to the Kennedys and the White House, coming and going as he liked. It was said he had his own room at the White House and did not need a security pass to enter the building as he wished. Jackie did not seem to object to this relationship with his old college friend, as Billings helped Kennedy to relax. Billings had accompanied Kennedy on his earlier European travels in the 1930s when they experienced the continent's rising tensions on the eve of the Second World War, but on this trip Billings described himself as 'the only civilian with absolutely no protocol status.'[22] He did though come in useful during the European tour when Kennedy needed a gift to present to the Pope in Rome and he sent Billings out to acquire a suitable item. Billing's closeness to Kennedy caused some annoyance amongst members of the administration; however, their friendship seemed to give Kennedy time-out from the stress of the demands of high political office.

The advance files suggest that Kennedy might have been accompanied by one of his sisters. Eunice and Jean, in fact, both came with him and were joined by Lee Radizwell, Jackie's sister, but no room in Brighton or at Birch Grove was formally allocated for them. It is possible that they went to London overnight with Lee Radizwell, where she lived in Buckingham Gate, rather than to the coast or Birch Grove.

The press contingent included many of the big name American journalists of the day: Edward Morgan, who later anchored ABC's coverage of the Kennedy Assassination; Sandy Vanocur of NBC, who covered Bobby Kennedy's assassination at the Ambassador Hotel in Los Angeles in 1968 and for the regional papers, Wilfrid Rodgers, of the 'Boston Globe'. Peter Lisagor, Washington bureau chief of the 'Chicago Daily News' and Bruce Rothwell of the 'New York Post' all covered the trip, staying at the Metropole. 'Time Magazine's' Hugh Sidley travelled on the trip too, also staying at the Metropole. The White House Press Corps took a twin bedded room at the Crown public house, close to Birch Grove, presumably to enable a couple of journalists to stand-by at the house overnight.

As at Gatwick Airport, 30 sound proof booths were set up in the Metropole for press use. These were coin operated, and worked with the assistance of the Post Office. Teleprinters were also installed to ensure quick access to the news wires. The near 100 assembled members of the press in Brighton, however, had little fresh news to cover until the scheduled press appearances at Birch Grove on Sunday morning. A press briefing took place in the Metropole at 8pm on the Saturday and after filing stories for the Sunday editions back in the US, they too had a relaxing evening in Brighton. If they were looking for something to do, they were in luck as Brighton Corporation, then the local council, had even prepared a special guide to the resort for each visitor, with details of how they might enjoy spending the evening in the town. The guide was left in each of their hotel rooms.

Chapter Five

In his diaries, Macmillan recounts the anticipation and excitement Kennedy's visit caused in the local area, painting a romantic picture of his arrival at Birch Grove:

> 'From the very first moment when the President's helicopter flew in and landed in the park until his departure there was a feeling of excitement combined...I can see him now, stepping out of the machine, this splendid, young, gay figure, followed by his team of devoted adherents.'[23]

Macmillan stated that whilst their arrival was late, the rest of the timings went more or less as planned. Once he had settled in, Kennedy had an opportunity to recover from the strain of the previous few days on the road; during such moments of respite he would usually have a hot bath to relieve his back pain. Back pain had dogged Kennedy throughout his life. Publicly said to be caused by his war wounds, it is now known that it was due to his Addison's disease. By that stage of his Presidency Kennedy was taking drugs, such as cortisone, to relieve the pain. As a result, Jacqueline Kennedy said that he had never been fitter,[24] and Macmillan recalled that '...none of these disabilities seemed to have the slightest effect upon his temperament'.[25] Before dinner, Kennedy was then due to begin the private talks with Macmillan.

Dinner at Birch Grove was scheduled to take place at 8pm. Macmillan and Kennedy sat down with a small group – including Rusk, Bundy and Ambassador David Bruce for the Americans, and Lords Home and Hailsham and Sir David Ormsby-Gore for the British. Macmillan presented Kennedy with the gift of a pair of china blue jay birds, made by the Crown Pottery in Staffordshire. Dorothy Macmillan and their son and daughter-in-law joined the dinner, cooked by Macmillan's housekeeper, Mrs Bell and the few servants they had who Macmillan later recounted had 'excelled'. Kennedy presented Lady Dorothy with a dressing table set as a token of his appreciation for their hospitality. Writing from Washington on his return, Kennedy thanked Macmillan for the dinner, saying the meals at Birch Grove would 'make my wife ask if the cook would like to live in the United States'. The dinner would have been a precursor to the talks the next day, with a less formal atmosphere than the official discussions between world leaders that would follow.

Mrs Bell and her sleeping arrangements for the visit briefly took centre stage in the house and in Downing Street. A memo between de Zulueta and the Prime Minister prior to Kennedy's arrival requested that Lady Dorothy Macmillan approach Mrs Bell to consider moving bedrooms, to accommodate Kennedy's chief security officer, so that he could be in the room adjacent to the President, 'on the assumption of course that Lady Dorothy would be able to ask Mrs Bell to move upstairs for the night'.

Ahead of the visit, Kennedy had expressed his desire to spend time in the Sussex countryside and a visit to Macmillan's Birch Grove estate gave him the perfect opportunity for this. After the dinner, locals have suggested that he visited the nearby Chelwood Gate public house, where some of his Secret Service detail stayed. The pub, adjacent to the Birch Grove estate was one of the communication centres used during the visit. Now called the Red Lion, the pub still references itself as

Macmillan's and Kennedy's local. The police log does not show any movements outside the estate in the evening, so the story remains one of those little local intrigues that make the visit so fascinating.

The next morning, Kennedy's unusually small motorcade, without police outriders, left Birch Grove to attend the 8.30am mass at the Our Lady of the Forest church in Forest Row, driving through four miles of narrow country lanes. This presented the public with their only opportunity to view the President during his visit and crowds packed the narrow country lanes to try and glimpse him, giving the East Sussex Constabulary its only serious headache of the visit, and indeed, their own brief moment in the spotlight.

The East Sussex Police had been preparing for the visit since early June, with Chief Constable, R. Berefit taking personal charge of the policing arrangements. Berefit had written to the Home Office asking if the Prime Minister would, in return, write to him requesting personal protection for the visit, a request rejected by the Home Office with some puzzlement. Taking no risks, Berefit drew over 200 police officers from across the south of England and as far as Lewisham in south London, 'draining' police resources from across the region. Those officers from outside the county were sworn-in by three magistrates who also stood-by during the visit at the request of Berefit, who literally left no stone unturned in his preparations. The WVRS and Red Cross supported his officers, and many stayed at the Isle of Thorns and Maresfield camps in the nearby forest, where the officers were reported to have drunk the bar dry the night before.[26] The Police also secured the Brighton communication sites, closing the seafront road to ensure speedy access between the landing site and hotels. Berefit can perhaps be seen as an old fashioned police chief, typical of the day, ensuring that every detail of the visit was covered and that no unexpected problems would arise whilst the President was on his patch.

One set of police officers from Crawley, then of the neighbouring Surrey Constabulary, failed to arrive in time getting delayed en route, however it probably mattered little as the local police were as much bystanders in the visit as the sightseers who had flocked to see the President driving through the country lanes on his way to the church that morning. Crawley police officer, John Molyneux recalls the farce which followed:

> 'They went to early morning service at Forest Row church and although they were accompanied by numerous armed police we were to follow them in our coach. The coach was clapped out and under powered, so that by the time they reached the church, a distance of about three miles, we were just crossing the forest and never reached Forest Row. The whole episode seems to have been organised, not by a gold or silver commander, but by a white metal alloy ranking officer!'[27]

During the short journey to the church, protestors again took the opportunity to make their point about nuclear testing, which Macmillan records that Kennedy took in a good-natured way. The demonstrations at Birch Grove had caused increasing concern with the Home Office and police, and there must have been some relief that no problems were caused by the presence of the protest. Indeed footage shows Kennedy looking relaxed and enjoying the drive through the countryside that summer morning. As Dave Powers had not made it there from Brighton from the night before, Macmillan's Private Secretary, Sir Philip de Zulueta joined Kennedy in the car. Earlier in June, Pierre Salinger undertook an advance visit to the church, and had asked the local priest, Father Charles Dolman not to preach a sermon. Dolman duly obliged just delighted that 'one of the world's leading Catholics should be with us in our little wayside chapel this morning'.[28] Five seats in the church were made available to the press, but not for photographers, whilst other worshippers needed special tickets from the priest to gain admittance. 'The Times' on 1st July tells the story of Kennedy's brief Sunday morning excursion…

> 'For two all-too-fleeting moments, in ... Forest Row, Mr. Kennedy was seen today on his way to and from Mass by hundreds of villages lining the lanes that led to the Church of our Lady of the Forest. From before 7 a.m. there were people waiting, television cameras on the roof tops, security men under every bush....
>
> Suddenly down the lane came two of the most enormous Cadillacs that anyone had ever seen. Car GG300, from "the nation's capital, District of Columbia" came first with the President, smiling and waving under a glass roof, followed by GG 308, full of enormous men with crew hair cuts.
>
> The President went into church for the ticket-only service and sat, as is apparently his custom, in the

centre of the congregation with a security man on either side, one in front and one behind....

The service lasted 40 minutes and then Father Charles Dolman escorted the President to his car. Just as though it looked as though the crowd had seen the last of Mr Kennedy, there came the best touch of the day.

The President suddenly jumped out of the car and walked briskly towards the cheering crowd, who were a little fed up with security by this time.

"Oh, my God, he's done it again", said a horrified bodyguard, leaping from his seat like a stricken rabbit. By now Mr. Kennedy was shaking hands with everyone in sight. It lasted only a minute, but it won everyone over...."

GG300 was Kennedy's official Cadillac, flown into the UK especially for the visit as part of the arrival convoy at Gatwick the day before. Known as X-100 or SS-100-X by the Secret Service, it is the car which Kennedy used most often during his Presidency, including on the day of his assassination in Dallas. The 1961 Lincoln Continental was leased to the US government by the Ford Motor Company and even after the assassination the vehicle was modified to improve security and subsequently used on occasions by Presidents Johnson, Nixon, Ford and Carter. The First Lady's Secret Service Agent Clint Hill described the midnight blue limosine as the 'most advanced' Presidential vehicle of its kind at the time.[29] It included a hydraulic lift to allow the President and First Lady to be lifted by over a foot to enable the crowds to get a better view. It even had a loudspeaker, should the President feel the need to make a speech. Two bubble-top Cadillacs were flown in for the visit, with one British Rolls Royce also standing by. Little did the locals realise that the scene of Kennedy driving through the Sussex countryside that quiet Sunday morning would be so similar to those historic images in Dallas just a few months later.

In a precursor to today's fast-moving political communications, the President took his communications with him wherever he went. Kennedy and his entourage were rarely away from a fixed White House telephone communication link, even during his excursion to the church. A pair of secure telephone wires were laid between the church and a policeman's house opposite, enabling the President's security detail to remain in touch with those at the main house and indeed if needed the wider world. In the days before blackberries and mobile phones, the physical planning for his communications was immense.

Locals still talk about his trip to mass that Sunday: the child challenged by the police for having a toy gun, the crowds of school children lining the route to glimpse the President and the press perched on nearby rooftops to get the best photographs of him. Macmillan notes that the weather on the Sunday was better than the wet Saturday, with a 'lovely afternoon' in store for the visitors. As he passed through those country lanes, Kennedy would be seeing the Sussex countryside at its summertime best, and indeed the watchers, sightseers and protestors in return saw Kennedy at his most relaxed and at the top of his political game.

The police log notes that Macmillan went to church separately in Horsted Keynes, leaving Birch Grove at 8.35am. Macmillan attended the beautiful Anglican parish church, St Giles in the village where he and his family members are now buried. Kennedy returned to Birch Grove at 9.30am and the police log records that there were 'no disturbances' on his arrival back. The next entry in the log is for 4.08pm, nearly an hour after his scheduled departure when Kennedy left for Gatwick to depart the UK. In the meantime, after a short photo call with the press on the terrace of Birch Grove House, the scene was set for six hours of talks.

Chapter Six

Kennedy and Macmillan had developed a deep personal friendship during their previous meetings and were easily the closest of the world leaders at that time. The elder Macmillan perhaps saw himself as mentor to the younger Kennedy, who charmed the elder statesman with his relaxed, new world style and laid-back approach. Indeed, there was also a closeness between them as both men's lives crossed through their family connections. It is easy to dismiss the two as coming from different ages and times, but, whilst that is true, they also had much in common. They both came from aristocratic backgrounds with strong parentage: Joseph P. Kennedy and Nellie Macmillan, in their differing ways, played major roles in each of their son's lives. By the time of Birch Grove, both men wanted to move the political agenda forward, Kennedy in the shadow of the Bay of Pigs and Cuban Missile Crisis, Macmillan in the face of declining domestic popularity. Both men had the prospect of a forthcoming election ahead of them, although they would be elections neither would go onto fight.

What is clear is that Macmillan adored Kennedy, writing in his memoirs about him almost as he would of a son. In her recorded tapes in 1964, Jacqueline Kennedy agreed, saying that 'Jack had this high sense of mischief and so did Macmillan, so I've never seen two people enjoy each other so.'[30] Presidential historian, Robert Dallek echoes this by saying that 'Macmillan's intelligence and dry, quick wit had delighted the President.'[31] The letters and telegrams they exchanged throughout their time in office were always addressed 'dear friend', and the telephone recordings show a deep genuine friendship between them.

In his memoirs, Macmillan described the scene at Birch Grove that morning:

> 'Inside the house it seemed more like a play or rather the mad rehearsal for a play, than a grave international conference. There was none of the solemnity which usually characterises such meetings. After all, we were all friends and many of us intimate friends; and the whole atmosphere was that of a country house party... There seemed a perpetual flow of diplomats and politicians and their staffs.'

In mid June, Macmillan approved an advanced list of items for discussion, which included the issues around nuclear testing, the multilateral force, British Guiana, the European political scene and Laos and the Far East, 'generally'. Briefings were provided to Macmillan on each item, with de Zulueta expecting the nuclear test talks to take precedent. The discussion items, especially relating to the handover of British Guiana, reflected the decline of Britain's post-war colonial power and, with it, America's rising assertion in the Far East. They also reflected the instability of mainland Europe, especially in the light of Kennedy's earlier visit to Berlin. From the start, Macmillan took personal control over the content of the talks, which Kennedy seemed relaxed enough to allow:

> 'All the serious discussions took place between him and me alone, with sometimes Private Secretaries to record discussions. This seemed to be much the most effective way for reaching rapid and full agreement. But at the end of the

> day I suggested that since this mass of experts had been assembled…we really ought to give them a show.'[32]

Macmillan clearly adored his role as host. He also enjoyed having as much time as he could for his private talks with Kennedy, keeping others hanging around the house, waiting to be called in when needed. When eventually brought in by Macmillan, they were used almost as a question and answer panel, with the two leaders drawing on their views. However, it seems from Macmillan's point of view at least, that the significant progress was made on a one-to-one basis with Kennedy.

The main item of discussion was the emerging opportunity for a partial nuclear test ban treaty. The treaty would limit nuclear testing in the atmosphere, underwater or in space and was seen as one of the successes of the Kennedy-Macmillan partnership, and of both men's periods in office. Macmillan was keen to see the pursuit and conclusion of any subsequent agreement as a joint success, something he could take credit for against the difficult domestic backdrop. Although initially dismissed by Kennedy and Rusk at Birch Grove as unattractive to the Russians, a consensus would emerge between the powers for a partial ban, with the intention of slowing the arms race, rather than stopping it. By that stage Khrushchev had softened his position on a partial ban, with only the question of enforcement and inspections remaining. By 15th July 1963, a three way meeting was held between Russia, America and Britain to take forward the partial ban, which was later signed in the autumn. France, North Korea and China did not sign the treaty and continued their nuclear testing programmes. Writing in his diary, Macmillan noted that at Birch Grove, 'we got what we wanted' with 'full steam ahead' on the Moscow talks on the nuclear issue.[33]

Kennedy and Macmillan's country house diplomacy provided the vital building blocks for achieving the historic partial test ban. It also allowed the continuation of discussions on American proposals for a 'multi-lateral force' manned by NATO, although this proposal found less consensus between the British and Americans. The plan, pursued by the US since the Eisenhower administration was causing concern in the UK and would not emerge as a serious proposition for the British. Kennedy aide and court historian, Arthur Schlesinger, in his book 'A Thousand Days, John F. Kennedy in the White House' wrote that 'Macmillan said no on the multilateral force and yes on British Guiana.'[34] There was also light relief during the meeting, with Macmillan recalling a joke between Kennedy and himself to allow the Russians to join the multilateral force, a proposition that did not amuse their aides, but gentle leg pulling which delighted Macmillan.

John McNaughton, General Counsel of the US Department of Defence, US State Department, records the talks as follows:

> 'The President and the Prime Minister with their advisers discussed test ban matters during a meeting at Birch Grove from 11:45 a.m. until 1:15 p.m., Sunday, June 30 1963. Present at the discussions assisting the President were Secretary Rusk, Ambassador Bruce, and Messrs. Tyler, McNaughton, and Long. Assisting the Prime Minister, in addition to his personal secretary, were Lord Home (in and

out), Minister Thorneycroft, Ambassador Ormsby-Gore, [and] Lord Hailsham....

The Prime Minister asked "the scientists" to provide the answers to the three questions put to them the night before. I read to them the questions and in each case the answers which had been prepared ... There was discussion after each answer....

The President then read from the JCS June 18 "Comments on the Proposed Nuclear Test Ban Treaty." He read extensively from Parts II, III and IV of the JCS [Joint Chiefs of Staff] statement...The President stated that it will be important for us to "get back home and talk this over."

...Lord Home suggested that, in the Moscow negotiations, we should not permit the debate to focus on number of inspections. Rather, he preferred to have the emphasis put on kinds of inspection.

There was some discussion of what inducements the Soviets might have to agree to a test ban. In response to a question from Lord Hailsham, I said that the interest on the part of the Soviets might flow (1) from a different strategic outlook (one in which superiority in very large weapons appeared sufficient), and (2) from a desire to prevent proliferation of nuclear weapons capabilities. The Prime Minister added two reasons: (3) That the Soviets may wish to save the resources now being diverted to the arms race, and (4) that they may be interested in taking a step toward disarmament. He doubted very much that the Soviets would enter a treaty intending to cheat; he believed that the question in their minds would be "Do we want this deal or don't we?" The questions would be how much each side had to give to reach agreement.

The President raised the question of a partial test ban—one which had no meaningful on-site inspections but which allowed a given number (possibly 7 to 10) of underground tests each year. He doubted that the Soviets would be interested in such a proposal. Secretary Rusk emphasized the importance for pressing for a comprehensive ban for quite some time before falling back to a partial ban. The President observed that such a partial ban would meet some of the Soviet needs while at the same time making a ban more consistent with US military and political requirements…'[35]

For the waiting press, the President and Prime Minister issued a joint communiqué, which highlighted their areas of agreement for the forthcoming Moscow talks on the Test Ban Treaty, the multi-lateral force and issues ranging from India, through to Laos.

Following lunch, by the Sunday afternoon the visit was drawing to a close with the formal talks completed. Macmillan movingly concluded his reminiscence of the President's stay at Birch Grove, by writing:

> 'Far too soon, the visit drew to an end. It was time to go. He went as he came, by helicopter…Hatless, with his brisk step, and combining that indescribable look of a boy on a holiday

with the dignity of a President and Commander-in-Chief, he walked across the garden to the machine. We stood and waved. I can see the helicopter now, sailing down the valley above the heavily laden, lush foliage of oak and beech at the end of June. He was gone. Alas, I was never to see my friend again. Before those leaves had turned and fallen he was snatched by an assassin's bullet from the service of his own country and the whole world.'[36]

Chapter Seven

Macmillan saw Kennedy that weekend at his most confident and most at ease in office: 'in the fall of 1963, Jack was at the top of his game, popular at home, respected overseas'.[37] Kennedy had come through the previous thousand days able to take his place on the world stage. Back home, he could begin to look to the 1964 election with more confidence than ever before.

It was, though, a brief moment in time. Both men would face unimaginable challenges in the days and months after Birch Grove. Kennedy returned to the United States in July on a wave of success following his European tour, but within just a few weeks, he faced the loss of his newly born son, Patrick, who died two days after birth on 7th August. The bereavement deeply moved Kennedy and the written exchanges between Macmillan and Kennedy illustrate the extent of concern Macmillan showed for his younger friend. Macmillan's time as Prime Minister was quickly running out. Hospitalised in October 1963, Macmillan resigned as Prime Minister, ending an administration dogged by scandal. Without the immediate need to call a General Election, Birch Grove participant Alec Douglas-Home was asked to form a government to complete the parliamentary term. One of his first acts would be the signing of the Partial Test Ban Treaty in October, for which Birch Grove had been such an important stepping-stone.

By November, Kennedy had an eye on re-election, and began reaching out to those states which had drifted from the Kennedy-Johnson fold since 1960, and whose support he would need in 1964 to secure re-election. Arriving in Dallas on November 22nd 1963, Kennedy received a rapturous welcome from the crowds, similar to those he saw in Berlin and Ireland on his European tour that summer. Later that day he was gunned down whilst driving through downtown Dallas. The scene of the smiling young President driving through Dallas that day could, perhaps, bring to mind the Sunday morning drive that summer through the Sussex countryside just a few months earlier.

The assassination of John F. Kennedy was one of the most momentous events of the twentieth century. It denied America of one its great leaders. It denied history the answer to so many questions: would Kennedy have won in 1964; would he have committed fully to the escalating conflict in Vietnam and would he have acted on his domestic agenda. Speaking movingly days later in the House of Commons, Harold Macmillan spoke of his personal grief at the loss of his friend. He said:

> 'President Kennedy was a man of the highest physical and moral courage, tested and proved in war and in peace. When things were difficult, almost desperate, he was both resourceful and resolute. When things seemed a bit easier, he displayed a boyish and infectious delight which was irresistible. Although his career has been cut short so tragically, he will stand high even among the great names of great American Presidents…
>
> We mourn for him and for his bereaved family, to whom we offer our respectful sympathy, and for all the American people; and we mourn him—and this

> is perhaps the greatest tribute to Jack Kennedy's life
> and work—for ourselves, for what we and all the
> world have lost.'

In the years that followed, both Chelwood Gate and Forest Row would mark the visit of President Kennedy. Jacqueline Kennedy herself visited Birch Grove to call on Harold Macmillan, who by which time had been widowed himself after the loss of his wife, Dorothy. Ethel Kennedy would also visit Macmillan there too, after the death of her husband, Robert Kennedy during the 1968 primary campaigns. President Kennedy's brother, Senator Edward Kennedy met with Macmillan in London the year after the assination.

Harold Macmillan lived in retirement until his death in 1986, and whilst John F. Kennedy was buried in the spectacular surroundings of Arlington Cemetery, overlooking the Lincoln Monument and Washington DC, Macmillan is buried in a quiet near forgotten plot at his local parish church, St Giles, just down the road from his beloved Birch Grove.

In the villages of rural East Sussex, John F. Kennedy's brief visit is still remembered to this day.

Epilogue – National Archives File CAB 21/5559/1 Closed Extract: Brief 13

The air of Cold War mystery still surrounds one element of the visit. This history of the events of that June weekend in 1963 benefitted enormously from files drawn from the UK National Archives, John. F. Kennedy Library, US State Department and those of the East Sussex Records Office. Of all the requests for files and for assistance in writing a comprehensive account of the arrangements of the visit, one fell on deaf ears and was repeatedly blocked by officials: that of the 'UK National Archives File CAB 21/5559/1 Closed Extract: Brief 13' the contents of which remain a mystery at the time of writing. The UK government persists in denying access to the file, which, it is believed, relates directly to the Kennedy-Macmillan foreign discussions during the weekend, and possibly relating to Jordan. However, as the government declassified the other files relating to the visit early, this raises questions about the contents of this particular file. Indeed, repeated requests and appeals under the Freedom of Information Act have produced negative outcomes, and just an apology for refusing to open the file according to procedure.

Appendix 1: Joint Communiqué: Birch Grove House, Sunday, 30th June, 1963.

During the past two days President Kennedy and Prime Minister Macmillan have held their seventh meeting to discuss current problems. Their talks have taken place at Prime Minister Macmillan's home in Sussex and followed on President Kennedy's visit to Germany and Eire. The United States Secretary of State, Mr. Rusk, Lord Home, British Foreign Secretary, Mr. Duncan Sandys, Secretary of State for Commonwealth Relations and Secretary of State for the Colonies, Lord Hailsham, Lord President of the Council, Mr. Thorneycroft, Minister of Defence, and Mr. Heath, Lord Privy Seal, took part in the talks at various times.

During some twelve hours of discussion the President and the Prime Minister began by hearing reports from Lord Home and Mr. Rusk about conversations which the two Ministers had held in London during the previous two days. The topics covered included Laos and the Far Eastern situation, the position in the Middle East, the problems of N.A.T.O. and the Western alliance and the effort for a test ban treaty. President Kennedy and the Prime Minister took note in particular of the situation in Laos and expressed their concern at the frequent breaches of the Geneva Agreement of 1962 and at the failure of certain parties to the Agreement to carry out their obligations under it. They agreed to continue to work closely together for the preservation of peace in Laos and the independence and neutrality of that country. They also agreed to continue close general co-operation in the Far East, particularly in regard to the problems of Vietnam. As regards the Middle East, the President and the Prime Minister agreed on the importance of the efforts made by the United Nations in working towards conciliation in the Yemen and pledged their support to the Secretary-General.

The President and the Prime Minister were agreed on their policy of continuing to help India by providing further military aid to strengthen her defences against the threat of renewed Chinese-Communist attack. They were impressed by the importance to the economic progress and defence of both India and Pakistan of whose anxieties they were fully aware, of an honourable and equitable settlement of the outstanding differences between the two countries; they stood ready to help in any way which might be desired by both countries.

President Kennedy and the Prime Minister then reviewed the problems of the Western Alliance especially in regard to N.A.T.O. They noted with satisfaction the decisions reached at the recent N.A.T.O. meeting in Ottawa which implemented the concept which they had themselves set out at their meeting at Nassau in December, 1962, by which a number of powers assigned some or all of their present and future forces to N.A.T.O. Command. With regard to the future they took note of the studies now under way in N.A.T.O. for review of the strategic and tactical concepts which should underlie N.A.T.O.'s military plans.

The President reported on his discussions with Dr. Adenauer in which they reaffirmed their agreement to use their best efforts to bring into being a multilateral sea-borne M.R.B.M. force and to pursue with other interested governments the principal questions involved in the establishment of such a force.

The President and the Prime Minister agreed that a basic problem facing the N.A.T.O. Alliance was the closer association of its members with the nuclear deterrent of the Alliance. They also agreed that various possible ways of meeting this problem should be further discussed with their allies. Such discussions would include the proposals for a multilateral sea-borne force, without prejudice to the question of British participation in such a force.

The President and the Prime Minister also reviewed the state of East-West relations and considered in particular the possibility of concluding in the near future a treaty to ban nuclear tests. They agreed that the achievement of such a treaty would be a major advance in East-West relations and might lead on to progress in other directions. They agreed the general line which their representatives, Mr. Averell Harriman and Lord Hailsham should take during their visit to Moscow in July. The President and the Prime Minister reaffirmed their belief that the conclusion of a test ban treaty at this time is most urgent and pledge themselves to do all they could to bring this about.

Birch Grove, Sussex. 30th June, 1963

Appendix 2: Arrival remarks by President Kennedy at Gatwick Airport, 29 June, 1963.

For Immediate Release   June 29, 1963

OFFICE OF THE WHITE HOUSE PRESS SECRETARY
(Brighton, England)

THE WHITE HOUSE

REMARKS OF THE PRESIDENT
UPON ARRIVAL AT GATWICK AIRPORT,
GATWICK, ENGLAND

Prime Minister, I am delighted to have this opportunity to meet with you again. I believe this is our seventh meeting we have had in various parts of the world. But though the geography has changed on different occasions, the subject that we have dealt with have been very much the same; that is, how we can organize our life here in the West, our relations between our countries and those associated with us, so that our people will find themselves living in a more fruitful and productive world, and also in a world of peace and freedom. That was, of course, the challenge which you and my predecessor discussed together in the 50's, and which we now discuss in the 60's.

I am particularly glad on this occasion that we will have an opportunity to talk about the forthcoming trip of our representatives to the Soviet Union. If we could ever bring some degree of control over nuclear matters to the world, I think we would decide that not only had all our other meetings been most useful, but all efforts that have been made in both our countries for so many years for peace and for order, and for sense of security – all this effort would be more than justified.

And I am particularly glad, also Prime Minister, to have an opportunity to visit you in your home. I am very glad to be back in England again.

Thank you.

END

Appendix 3: Departure remarks by President Kennedy at Gatwick Airport, 29 June, 1963.

For Immediate Release   June 30, 1963

OFFICE OF THE WHITE HOUSE PRESS SECRETARY
(Gatwick, England)

THE WHITE HOUSE

REMARKS OF THE PRESIDENT
UPON DEPARTURE AT GATWICK AIRPORT,
GATWICK, ENGLAND

Prime Minister, I want to express our very warm thanks to you and to Lady Dorothy for the shelter you have given us during the last 24 hours. As usual, we were able to accomplish a good deal in this meeting because of the strong basis of understanding which has existed between our two countries and which has existed to my great satisfaction since the period of my incumbency.

The most important matter, of course, which occupies our attention, is our common hope that the mission of Governor Harriman and Lord Hailsham will be successful, and I think the progress that we made during our discussions in coming to an agreement on the instructions of our emissaries, I think, made this meeting particularly useful.

So from public and personal grounds both, I wish to express our warmest thanks to you, and to tell you that we look forward to your visiting the United States next time around.

END

Appendix 4: Harold Macmillan's comments in the House of Commons, 2 July 1963.

Extract from Hansard

PRESIDENT KENNEDY (MEETING)

HC Deb 02 July 1963 vol 680 cc198-9

Q7 Mr A. Henderson

asked the Prime Minister whether he will make a statement on his recent meeting with President Kennedy.

Q9 Mr A. Lewis

asked the Prime Minister if he will make a statement on his recent official discussions with the President of the United States; and to what extent matters connected with security were raised during these talks.

Q14 Mr Rankin.

asked the Prime Minister if he will make a statement on the result of his talks with President Kennedy.

The Prime Minister

I would refer the right hon. and learned and hon. Gentlemen to the joint communiqué issued after my talks with President Kennedy. I will arrange for this to be circulated in the OFFICIAL REPORT.

Mr Henderson

Can we take it from the terms of the communiqué that in the event of a successful outcome of the talks in Moscow leading to an agreement for the banning of nuclear tests, President Kennedy and the Prime Minister are in agreement that that will be followed by a meeting with Mr. Khrushchev to deal with outstanding problems?

The Prime Minister

I know the right hon. and learned Gentleman's keen interest in these matters, and he knows mine. While we must not be too optimistic, we must struggle hard to get the result we want. Should we get it, great opportunities will, of course, open up—for all of us.

Mr A Lewis

I have seen the communiqué but there is no reference in it to any question of security. Can the right hon. Gentleman say whether or not he mentioned to the President recent security cases in this country, with particular reference to the Philby case? Is it because of that case, and the stories circulating in the American Press, that the Lord Privy Seal made his statement yesterday? Or did the Prime Minister not think it worth while having discussions on this matter?

The Prime Minister

I am not prepared to reveal the character of the discussions I had with the President. The hon. Gentleman has shown his usual suspicion and lack of generosity in his approach to every problem.

Mr Rankin

Is the Prime Minister aware that yesterday the Daily Mirror said that he stood firm against Mr. Kennedy on the question of the mixed-manned force? Was that statement true or not?

Mr Speaker

Order. That question is out of Order.

Appendix 5: Exchange of messages between Kennedy and Macmillan in October 1963 upon the ratification of the Partial Test Ban Treaty:

Dear Friend,

This morning, as I signed the instrument of ratification of the Nuclear Test Ban Treaty, I could not but reflect on the extent to which your steadfastness of commitment and determined perseverance made this Treaty possible. Thanks to your never flagging interest, we were ready with our views when the Soviets decided they were ready to negotiate. If humanity is to be spared further radioactive contamination of the atmosphere, if the nuclear arms race is to be slowed down, if we are to make more rapid progress toward lasting stability in international affairs, it will be in no small measure due to your own deep concern and long labor. History will eventually record your indispensable role in bringing about the limitation of nuclear testing; but I cannot let this moment pass without expressing to you my own keen appreciation of your signal contribution to world peace.

With warm regards,
Sincerely,

JOHN F. KENNEDY
The White House
Washington DC
8th October, 1963

Dear Friend,

Very many thanks for your characteristically generous message about the Nuclear Test Ban Treaty. As you know I feel very deeply that it is the duty of our two countries to work together for world peace, by all means in our power. I have been very much sustained by the knowledge that you share this conviction as you have demonstrated so signally by your actions.

With warm regard,
Yours sincerely,

HAROLD MACMILLAN.
10 Downing Street, S.W.1,
8th October, 1963.[38]

Appendix 6: Tribute to President Kennedy in the House of Commons, 25 November 1963 by Harold Macmillan.

Extract from Hansard,

PRESIDENT KENNEDY (TRIBUTES)

HC Deb 25 November 1963 vol 685

3.50 p.m.

> Mr Harold Macmillan (Bromley)
>
> With the permission of the House I would like to add a few words to the eloquent tributes to the memory of President Kennedy which have been paid on behalf of all the three great parties in our country.
>
> My right hon. Friend the Foreign Secretary, and the right hon. Member for Smethwick (Mr. Gordon Walker) and the hon. Member for Huddersfield, West (Mr. Wade), who followed, have expressed in moving phrases the sympathy which we in the House, aye, and the whole people of Britain, feel with the people of the United States at this tragic moment in their history.

They have also made it abundantly clear that we here, and throughout the Commonwealth, share their sorrow to the full, for we do not merely mourn a grievous loss to the vigour and vitality of American public life; we mourn a world statesman, to whose leadership, in these critical but inspiring days, all the peoples of the world, of whatever race, creed or colour, looked with confidence and hope.

My only purpose in rising is to add a few sentences as a friend and, in a true sense, a colleague. For three years he and I worked in the closest association. Every few months we met—sometimes on British and sometimes on American soil—and in between we interchanged frequent messages and telephone talks. Anyone who knew the President could not fail to realise that behind the captivating charm of manner lay an immense fund of deeply pondered knowledge on a wide range of subjects—political, economic, military. He was one of the best-informed statesmen whom it has ever been my lot to meet, but he was altogether without pedantry or any trace of intellectual arrogance.

The President was very fond of asking questions and trying to find out other people's views. He was chary of giving his own opinion except after much reflection and consideration. Admirably briefed as he always was by his staff, he never stuck slavishly to a brief. Unlike some men with whom discussion is often almost a formality, he was always ready to listen to and to be convinced by argument. In this way he brought to the baffling problems of today a remarkable freshness of mind and flexibility of approach. These were based upon his fundamental moral and mental integrity.

President Kennedy was a man of the highest physical and moral courage, tested and proved in war and in peace. When things were difficult, almost desperate, he was both resourceful and resolute. When things seemed a bit easier, he displayed a boyish and infectious delight which was irresistible. Although his career has been cut short so tragically, he will stand high even among the great names of great American Presidents.

In this country we shall always remember him its a sincere and loyal friend of Britain. To the whole world without distinction his life and words and actions were a constant inspiration. He did not regard it as a statesman's duty to yield to public opinion, but to strive to lead it. Subjected to great pressures on many conflicting issues, he seemed sometimes to be almost a rather lonely figure, but always true to his own integrity and his own faith. What he said, he meant, and he did his best to accomplish. To him the words "peace and progress" were not just a phrase for a peroration, but a living and burning faith.

So it was, as has been said already, that when that terrible news came on Friday everyone in this country—and, I think, in every country—felt stunned by the shock of what seemed to us—to each one of us—a personal bereavement, and to the whole of humanity, struggling in this world of darkness, the sudden and cruel extinction of a shining light.

We mourn for him and for his bereaved family, to whom we offer our respectful sympathy, and for all the American people; and we mourn him—and this is perhaps the greatest tribute to Jack Kennedy's life and work—for ourselves, for what we and all the world have lost.

Hon. Members

Hear, hear.

Acknowledgements

In putting this history together, I was grateful for the assistance of a number of archivists who helped me to access the original files relating to the visit. These included those from the UK National Archives, John F. Kennedy Library in Boston, Massachusetts and the East Sussex Records Office in Lewes. Online files were also accessed from the UK National Archives, US State Department, JFK Library, House of Commons and the Ford Museum in Detroit. At times reading these files and the incredible depth of information that they contained about the visit provided a fascinating and exciting first-hand journey through the events of June 1963.

Cover photograph courtesy of American Nostalgia, with thanks. The political cartoon is by Victor Weisz, Evening Standard, 28th July 1963, with thanks.

I am grateful to the House of Commons for the Hansard extracts, I felt it was important to reproduce both in the text and full in the Appendix Macmillan's tribute to President Kennedy in November 1963, as the best way to conclude this short history and express the strength of feeling at the time.

I am also grateful for local history websites for highlighting 'The Times' article of the 1 July 1963. I also felt that this was best reproduced in its entirety as part of the main text.

One of the hardest elements of writing this short history is the amount of folklore that has evolved around the visit. There has been a considerable blurring of memories over the facts of the visit, ranging from how Kennedy's blood was stored, whether he went for an evening drink in the local pub and even if Macmillan and Kennedy discussed their sex lives! I've avoided as much of this as possible, rooting each point I made on the three government files I extensively used. Fact though is often more interesting than fiction.

Finally, I don't expect this to be a great work of literature, but more the re-telling of a short story sometimes forgotten by the history books. In putting it together I am grateful for both the professional and informal advice received, and any mistakes contained here are my own and for which I take responsibility.

Paul Elgood
paulelgood@gmail.com
June 2012

About the author

Paul Elgood has studied all UK and US elections since the late eighties. He witnessed at first hand Teddy Kennedy's final Senate campaign in Massachusetts in 2006 and Barack Obama's Presidential election victory in 2008, standing in Chicago's Grant Park with 180,000 others to see Obama accept the Presidency.

He has a degree in American history and politics from York St John and lives in Hove, East Sussex.

Notes on file sources

Three original files from the time, were used as the major sources of this history, namely:

Master file on operations SPA/2/26/15, Jun - Aug 1963: held by the East Sussex Records Office, Lewes which includes: Copy of operational order giving programme, plans of area, details of press arrangements etc; control log of incidents and message forms; sample passes, declarations of special constables, chief constable's report and accounts of the cost of the operation, correspondence with other forces on collaboration, letters of thanks including one from the Prime Minister, original of cartoon by Gus in the Evening News based on security aspects of the visit.

Records of the Cabinet Office, Visit by President Kennedy to UK, June 1963 CAB 21/5559, 1963 June-July: held by the UK National Archives, Kew.

Trips: United Kingdom, June 1963: 29-30: held by the JFK Library, Boston, this folder contains materials collected by the office of President John F. Kennedy's secretary, Evelyn Lincoln concerning President Kennedy's trip to Great Britain. Materials in this folder include itineraries, newspaper articles, a telegram welcoming the President to England, and letters of thanks for courtesies extended to the President.

Occasionally I have not made direct a reference in the text as it will relate to a source from one of these three files, depending on the subject.

The other main source is Harold Macmillan's own account in his diaries, published in 'At the End of the Day', 1973.

End Notes

[1] Harold Macmillan, *At The End of the Day,* 473
[2] O'Donnell/Powers *Johnny We Hardly Knew Ye*, 361
[3] Note – timings are drawn from three sources, using the one most relevant to the specific part of the trip and can slightly differ from those in his official White House diary extract for the visit.
[4] O'Donnell interviewed in *JFK in Ireland, Irish Times*
[5] *Ottawa Citizen*, June 27, 1963
[6] Kenneth Walsh, *Air Force One*, 64
[7] Figures from the US Embassy, London
[8] Will Smith, *The Kennedys amidst the Gathering Storm*, xxvi
[9] Ibid, 69
[10] Harold Macmillan, *At The End of the Day,* 473
[11] *Life Magazine*, June 9 1958
[12] Macmillan p471
[13] *The Times*, 1 July 1963
[14] Carol Milmo, *The Independent*, 27 Feb 2002
[15] Macmillan 472
[16] Ibid
[17] Ibid
[18] Gerald Blaine, *The Kennedy Detail*, 91
[19] Macmillan 472
[20] *New York Times*, 28 March 1998
[21] Bijal P. Trivedi, *National Geographic, The Kennedy Mystique,* 27 Feb 2004
[22] David Pitts, *Jack & Lem*, 223
[23] Macmillan, 472
[24] Jacqueline Kennedy, *Conversations*
[25] Macmillan, 474
[26] International Centre for the History of Crime, Policing and Justice - Surrey Constabulary 1961-1975
[27] Ibid
[28] Martin Beckford, *Daily Telegraph*, 21 December 2009
[29] Clint Hill, *Mrs Kennedy and Me*, 276
[30] Jacqueline Kennedy, *Conversations*, 215
[31] Robert Dallek, *John F. Kennedy An Unfinished Life,* p415
[32] Macmillan, 474
[33] Ibid, 472
[34] Arthur Schlesinger, *A Thousand Days*, 886
[35] US Department of State Archives: Foreign Relations of the United States, 1961-1963, Volume VII, Arms Control and Disarmament, document 306 Memorandum of conversation
[36] Macmillan, 474
[37] David Pitts, *Jack & Lem*, 224
[38] National Archives (UK): Records of the Cabinet Office, Cabinet: Memoranda, CAB 129/114, Papers: 101(63) - 186(63)

Printed in Great Britain
by Amazon.co.uk, Ltd.,
Marston Gate.